THE TREE

Marian Tumelty

THE TREE

A celebration of our living skyline

Edited by Peter Wood
Introduction by Richard Mabey

(In aid of the Woodland Trust)

DAVID & CHARLES
Newton Abbot   London

I dedicate THE TREE to my wife Lisa and the three 'Little-Woods'
Nicola, Katie, Laura. And to our families, branches everywhere.

OPPOSITE TITLE
The tree in the
landscape
CHARLIE WAITE

LEFT
Hawthorn berries
MARIAN TUMELTY

RIGHT
Great spotted woodpecker,
male and young
ERIC HOSKING

British Library Cataloguing in Publication Data
The Tree.
1. Visual arts. Special subjects: Trees
I. Wood, Peter
704.9434

ISBN 0-7153-9481-9

Typeset by Ace Filmsetting Ltd, Frome, Somerset

and printed in Singapore
by CS Graphics Pte Ltd

for David & Charles Publishers plc
Brunel House   Newton Abbot   Devon

CONTENTS

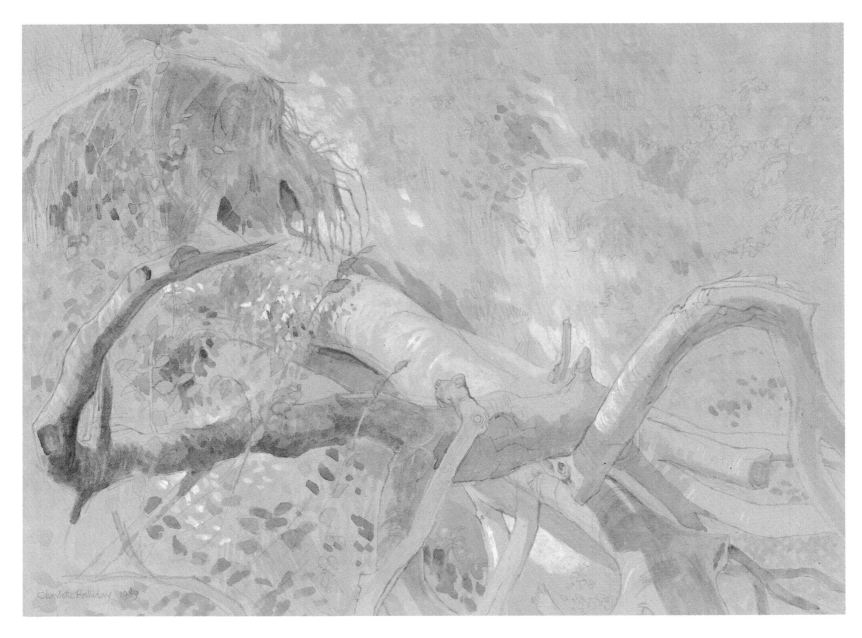

Victim of the hurricane: beech by the Arun CHARLOTTE HALLIDAY

FOREWORD

THE STORMS OF OCTOBER 1987 and January/February 1990 affected us all. After the terrible loss of human lives the most horrific loss was that of millions of trees. I wanted to do something special, something lasting in response. The seeds of an idea were germinated, and *The Tree* was born.

My idea was simple yet grand; to get together over 100 top artists, writers, photographers and the odd media personality who would be willing to donate work for use within THE ultimate celebration of trees and woodland.

I was lucky. Not only did I find a small band of supporters, I also attracted the attention of a publisher. My list of contributors grew, the publisher's enthusiasm grew and my work load grew and grew . . . !

It was always my intention that someone should benefit from *The Tree*, and The Woodland Trust was the obvious choice. The Trust's work of purchasing threatened woodlands always needs funds, so the book's royalties could prove very useful, especially when added to the funds raised by the sale of original works. (An exhibition and sale was also part of the master plan.)

The invitations were sent out to the cream of artistic talent and it soon became evident that trees are very important to many people. The response was incredible, the material outstanding.

Apart from raising funds for The Woodland Trust, *The Tree* has many aims. If you enjoy just one of the images, or if you are inspired to capture on film, paper or canvas your own view of our woodland heritage, it will have been a success. If you decide to plant a tree after viewing the beauty within these pages, or voice your concern the next time the bulldozers move in, better still.

There is something for everyone in this celebration. Turn each page slowly and savour, but never forget, *The Tree*.

Peter Wood.

The bulk of work to be found within *The Tree* is by professionals, but we felt that anyone with an artistic bent and love of trees would welcome the opportunity to take part. So, in conjunction with The Woodland Trust and *Practical Photography* magazine we ran two competitions, and the response to both was staggering.

The choice was difficult, but eventually we reached a decision, and five of the prizewinners are featured within. It is a tribute to the winners' skill that they fit so comfortably.

The Tree also attracted the attention of the Graphic Design Department of Newcastle Polytechnic, whose third year BA students used the idea for a project. In recognition of all the students' efforts we have chosen one of their pieces for inclusion.

ACKNOWLEDGEMENTS

THE TREE, like the subject it portrays, has taken a long time to reach fruition. It has also taken the time and talents of many companies and individuals. I would like to take this opportunity to thank:

All at David & Charles. Peter Stone and all at The Woodland Trust. Tony Crockford for words processed and otherwise. The Royal Mail for their assistance and safe deliveries. The Royal Photographic Society. *Practical Photography*. Gallery 5. Michael Spender (Royal Society of Painters in Watercolours). Chris Titherington (Department of Painting, Drawing and Photography Victoria and Albert Museum).

Those hardworking publicity departments at David & Charles, Walker Books, Paper Tiger, Kingfisher, Orchard Books, BBC Books and Andre Deutsch.

To anyone else I have forgotten, thank you, your help was much appreciated.

Finally, the biggest thank you must go to ALL our contributors who have given so generously of their time and talents to make this such a beautiful book. Thank you.

INTRODUCTION

I F WE HAD TO DESIGN from scratch the primary vegetation for the planet, to house and feed other living things, to regulate the cycles of air and water, it would be almost impossible to improve upon the trees. They are the architectural climax of evolution, the longest-lived organisms on earth, and even in their present depleted ranks still provide the world's greatest engine for converting the sun's energy into living tissue.

No wonder perhaps that trees have always been seen as a *challenge* by humans. Few people have been untouched, in some way, by their complexity and age and sheer stubborn rootedness. Early humans worshipped them; early farmers attacked them. In the Age of Improvement they were seen as expressions of national pride and social standing; in the Age of Industry as symbols of wasted land and rebellious spirits.

Today we are coming to respect the tree of life again. It is a full circle in more than one way, and a remarkable fusion of scientific and poetic vision. The ancient mythological idea of trees as the lungs of the earth is now known to be a hard ecological fact, and the struggle to save them is now a matter of urgent necessity as well as romantic affection.

The celebrations of trees collected in these pages – more than 100 works of art and writing – are a mark of our new response to that age-old challenge. Their depth and creativity give hope that the elder citizens of the earth and ourselves may yet be able to enjoy a common future.

Richard Mabey

Badgers, sow and cub MICK MANNING

10

Winter Elms, oil painting DAVID SHEPHERD

LEFT
Elm tree
MAURICE NIMMO

RIGHT
Bluebells under
beech trees
MAURICE NIMMO

TREE GARDENS

When walking the famous tree gardens of Levens Hall, Cumbria, it was quite something to behold the many different types of tree, shaped over the generations by its dedicated gardeners.

These leafy sculptures were quite an extraordinary sight to see. One a crown, another a castle; an archway and an armchair, a bird even. Fascinating. The one that impressed the eye the most was a mighty cedar. It was tree shaped.

PHIL COOL

Cedar Tree, an oil painting RICHARD BOX

An embroidered landscape THOMASINA BECK

Summer on the South Downs, Sussex
FRANK WOOTTON

TWENTY-FIVE YEARS AGO, I planted these plum trees in our garden. I have watched them grow. The first plum was an event. The trees spread, matured and gradually got in the way of the view into the hills. I didn't mind – blossom, leaves, fruit (often so much we had to let most of it rot on the tree), the dry, dark grid of their branches in winter – it was worth it.

Our cat climbs into the low branches to escape the next-door cat. Higher up, there are the birds: wood-pigeons, sparrows, starlings, blackbirds and thrushes. As the fruit ripens the trees buzz with insects.

In my painting I try to share this feeling of trees being a world in miniature, though they are really far from miniature. Shortly after I painted the picture, one of the trees blew down in a gale. Only when it lay on the ground and I had to cut it into pieces did I realise how big and complex a tree is.

HANS SCHWARZ

Plum Trees in our Somerset Garden HANS SCHWARZ

Black and white linocut BORIN VAN LOON

Treebeard (From *The Lord of the Rings* by J. R. R. Tolkien) RODNEY MATTHEWS

THE YEW IN THE CHURCHYARD

ALAN F. MITCHELL

THERE IS A BROAD CRESCENT encompassing parts of England and Wales in which there are giant yews in the churchyards of old parish churches. Only one really big yew, that at Keffolds near Haslemere in Surrey, is not associated with any known church or abbey. The crescent runs from Kent and Sussex to Dartmoor in Devon, round *via* Avon, Gloucestershire and Wiltshire to Gwent, Powys, Hereford and Clwyd to Shropshire and Derbyshire.

Several reasons for these trees being in churchyards have been suggested, but recent measurements and thinking have made a quite different solution much the most probable. There is no recorded tradition of planting a yew when the church was built, nor is this done today. Yews may be associated with immortality (with more reason, it now seems, than was appreciated); pollinating male branches were used on Palm Sunday, as they still are in Ireland; and yews must be kept away from grazing cattle and horses; so the churchyard was the place for them. They were also thought to have been grown for longbows, but in this country the yew is branchy and the wood is knotty. If the trunk were used for bows, there would not now be many old trees around, and, if only the branches were used, the signs of cutting them would be plain. Yews take a very long time to grow branches big enough to be useful, yet most churchyards have only one or two ancient yews. In fact, the longbows were made from staves attached as customs duty to casks of wine from Spain and Portugal.

The yew at Dryburgh Abbey, Selkirk, was planted in 1136. In 1894 it was 11ft 4in round and is now 12ft 6in – still small. So the one at Ulcombe in Kent (34ft 4in) and many others over 30ft, could be three or four times as old, or more. Re-measurement of many confirms exceedingly small increase with great age and suggests that these trees are around 3,000 years old. So the trees were there long before the Saxon church and Norman rebuilds. They were on holy ground, the tribal elders' meeting places, and the churches were built near them to take over the holy site and also to gain good shelter for their porches from wind and snow.

North door, St Edward,
Stow-on-the-Wold
DENNIS GILBERT

22

Coastal Trees Cornwall.   HC

Trees on a windy day by the cliffs of south Cornwall. 'Trees are
more difficult to draw than buildings. They don't stand still and
their intricate structure demands very careful study which few of
us are conscientious enough to undertake. To draw them well
you have to take trouble. My advice is Ruskin's, "Don't look at
them, watch them".'

HUGH CASSON

The quiet stream, Knapp Lane, Llangwm, Pembrokeshire MAURICE SHEPPARD

FIVE ELMS

JILLY COOPER

FOR TEN YEARS I walked my dogs on Putney and Barnes Commons in London, taking with me a notebook and trying to describe events and scenery as I saw them. One of my dogs was a very wild but utterly adorable English Setter called Maidstone, who tragically had to be put down because he killed so many cats.

My favourite trees were five beautiful elms on the north side of a winding stream. They were felled the same day Maidstone was put down, because they were regarded as a danger to the public. Here are some extracts describing them.

Friday, 23 February, 1973
An exquisite morning. Notice crimson blur on the five tallest elm trees on the the north side of Beverley Brook. On closer examination, I am enchanted to discover the blur is made up of tiny rose-pink flowers. Maidstone takes advantage of my studying nature to vanish. I comb the Common yelling. He is nowhere to be seen. In the end, as I have a *Sunday Times* piece to finish by the afternoon, I give up in despair and go home.

Thursday, 21 March, 1974
Take Maidstone out at dusk. In the copse near Barnes Graveyard a hawthorn is putting out leaves like tiny green flames. Down by the Brook, I find the first yellow celandine on the bank. Above, the starlings are gathering in my five beloved elms, blackening them against a soft lilac sky. In and out and round about the starlings wheel, with a high-pitched buzz, that can be heard for miles around. Maidstone runs down to the Brook, and gazes up at them with his mouth open and his speckled head on one side.

Monday, 1 April, 1974
Very warm – out without a jersey for the first time. Notice the poplars by the bowling green are thickening with scarlet catkins and bronze leaves. All the young greens are so beautiful: the saffron of the oaks, the buff of the planes, the pale jade of the willows, the acid green of the limes, and the darker inky green of my five lovely elms. But most beautiful of all is a pear tree in one of the back gardens of Lower Common South, which I can see from my study, moonlit green just before dawn, or dancing in the noon sunshine, its white garlanded arms rising and falling.

The blackthorn is already over and the colour of old lace. Progress round the Common is very slow, as Maidstone keeps getting plugged into vole holes.

Monday, 13 May 1974
A splendid row has broken out over the Common. In the middle of this perfect spring, the gas board has suddenly decided to lay a huge pipe, under Barnes Common, the Flower Garden, the two Hillocks, Beverley Brook, and down to the Thames. A big red crane already hangs like a malignant stork over my five tall elms. Today the workmen moved their bulldozers in, crashing through speedwell, buttercups and cow parsley, knocking down little hawthorns and oak trees in their green prime.

Even though I've only been walking on this Common for eighteen months, I feel all the outrage of a mother whose child has been raped.

Wednesday, 30 April, 1975
Beverley Brook is all white and bridal, choked with new cow parsley. A man on the opposite bank is examining my five beloved elms. To my horror, he tells me they are all dying of Dutch elm disease, and will soon have to come down. On closer examination, I see several of the branches are dead and not putting out green leaves any more. Feel desperately upset, and ask him how long he thinks they'll last.

He shrugs his shoulders, and says perhaps a year, perhaps more, but in the end all the elms along the Brook will have to come down.

Saturday, 18 October, 1975
I have started walking earlier in the morning to avoid dog fights, which means I sadly miss Rosie but happily see less of Rachel and Henrietta.

The acacia on the north-east of the Graveyard is still bluey-green, but tinfoil shavings of leaves on the ground show it is moulting too. Squirrels scatter as we walk through the Squirrel Wood. Each year I look forward to a view to the north of the Flower Garden, where above the pale blond grasses, and the amethyst Michaelmas daisies, my five lovely golding elms rise like the entwined masts of ships in a harbour. Is there any chance they will last for another autumn? On the Fair Triangle, where the trees are always ahead, a maple is blazing crimson and the sycamores are brilliant amber.

Thursday, 24 February, 1977
Lovely late afternoon walk after jolly lunch. The poplar on the corner of Putney Cemetery is saffron in the sunlight and filled with thrush song. The drained blue sky is criss-crossed with bright-pink aeroplane trails.

My shadow in the setting sun is twenty feet long and admirably thin. Two ducks fly out of the Brook, circle perfectly round the five tall elms, wings going like propellers, then set off swiftly one behind the other, but in perfect time. Their gleaming emerald heads match the little green shoots which are thrusting everywhere through the counterpane of dead leaves. The goose grass is already covered in little green bobbles.

Friday, 4 March, 1977
Exquisite day. Galloping dark blue clouds being blown across heavier white and grey clouds; the sun keeps appearing fleetingly, like a hostess coming into a second drawing-room, highlighting golden willows, coral roofs, and gilding brown tops of trees, and darting back again.

Must face fact that my five elms are dead, and their death will be more obvious when all the surrounding trees put out their leaves.

Thursday, 19 May, 1977
Outside it is still quite cold – two-sweater weather. My five elms – those sky-touching beauties – were felled the same day as Maidstone. In a way, their thundering crash was symbolic. They were cut down like him because they were dangerous and a liability. Their boles are pitted with holes from the wretched beetle. I remember them in their yellow glory in the autumn and how their pale pink flowers were always a first herald of spring.

I'm so sorry for the birds that nest there – it's like compulsory purchase; but somehow I don't feel things very much since Maidstone died.

The Brook looks different now that the elms are gone, like one of those slow-moving meandering Wiltshire rivers, flanked with osiers.

Sunday, 8 April, 1980
Slight frost. Clover leaves close up as though they are praying. Jays still crackling. Hear a bird singing exquisitely from a sycamore at Cat Corner near the first bridge. Am trying to identify it, when a woman in a camel-hair coat, with very dyed blonde hair, walks past me and suddenly cries out:

> *Oh to be in England*
> *Now that April's there,*
> *And whoever wakes in England*
> *Sees, some morning, unaware . . .*

'Can't remember the next bit, but that's the "wise thrush" over there,' she goes on, pointing to the pulsating sycamore.

> *. . . he sings each song twice over,*
> *Lest you should think he never could recapture*
> *The first fine careless rapture . . . !*

'That takes me back sixty years,' she continues. 'Can't remember how it goes on. Pity they don't teach poetry in schools today,' and she is off, high heels sinking into the wet grass.

I wander on, trying to think what comes after 'morning, unaware'. Suddenly I remember:

> *. . . unaware,*
> *That the lowest boughs and the brushwood sheaf,*
> *Round the elm-tree bole are in tiny leaf . . .*

But not any more . . . Oh, my elm trees and my Maidstone long ago!

(From *The Common Years* by courtesy of Methuen)

LEFT
Burning leaves ROSALIND KAYE
(2nd prize winner, Woodland
Trust Competition)

RIGHT
Sunset over single tree
EDMUND NAGELE

THE GREAT OAK

JOHN EBDON

MORE THAN FIFTY YEARS have passed since I made a tree-house between the spreading branches of the Great Oak in my father's garden on the Surrey/Hampshire borders.

Accessible only by a precarious retractable rope ladder it was to become my sanctuary from which, unseen, I could look down upon the world of grown-ups through its canopy of leaves. In common with most of my peers on the periphery of puberty I felt misunderstood by my elders; but within that haven I aired my private grievances to the grey squirrels and wood pigeons, and felt the better for it.

The Great Oak became part of my life. On leave from the RAF in the dark days of the war, I would climb into my bower as I did as a child, temporarily know peace of mind, and briefly feel secure before returning to fight in the air again. To me, the tree spelt stability. It epitomised the character of England and I felt that whilst it stood not all the might of Nazi Germany could conquer the soil in which it was rooted.

Years later after my parents had died and the house and its grounds had passed to me, the Great Oak became my children's private place in which they too shared their secrets and their sorrows. Sadly, my grandsons will never know that hidden paradise.

It was in the small hours of Friday, October 16th, 1987, that we heard the Great Oak's anguish above the hurricane-force winds which swept in from the sea and changed the landscape of Southern England; and when daylight broke we knew the worst.

The tree surgeons did a good job when they amputated the shattered limbs of the Great Oak, but as the chain-saw cut through its splintered branches and the cream pith cascaded around them, I felt it was part of me which was a-dying.

'We must plant another,' said my younger son whose garden centre had not escaped the havoc. 'Amen to that,' I said, 'so be it.'

RIGHT
Watercolour of oaks in
Bradgate Park, Leicester
ROBIN BELL CORFIELD

30

LEFT
Shelter and Tree
The shelter was built in a
wild place, using materials to
hand CHRIS DRURY

RIGHT
Early morning light on beeches,
Mark Ash, New Forest
HEATHER ANGEL

Weeping Willow, oil painting ALEX WILLIAMS

THE LEANING WILLOW

The spinney is long and narrow, threaded by a small stream. Its trees are mainly spindly ash, with some sycamore, hazel, holly and elder. By the stream are alder and a few old willow trees.

The undergrowth is a thick tangle of brier and bramble and giant nettles. Only at the eastern end, where the spinney meets the lane, are there trees of any virtue. Here stands on parade a well dressed rank of seven fine horse-chestnuts, their right hand marker a single beech.

Halfway along the southern fringe is a crab, whose little apples shone brightly in the autumn sunshine as we walked beneath it one late September morning.

Then we saw the fox.

He slipped into the far end of the spinney – a dog fox, by the size of him – but when we entered by the same gap, there was no sign of him, and though the three dachshunds marked his line eagerly, they lost scent and interest a little way in.

This scene was re-played on several walks, and always the dachshunds were at fault at the same place, beneath a big old crack-willow. As such trees often do, it leaned out over the stream, its thick trunk at an angle of 45 degrees to the ground.

We never found an earth in the spinney, so always presumed that the dog fox; on hearing or winding us, simply slid out on the far side and away.

Till one day as we stood beneath the willow, we chanced to look upwards. There he sat in a comfortable crotch fifteen feet up, paws together, brush curled neatly round him, ears pricked, looking down on us.

What a patronising look it was.

We left, feeling small.

The Leaning Willow HELEN CRAIG (Text by DICK KING-SMITH)

Wood mouse ALAN BEAUMONT

Beech tree
STEPHEN DALTON

RIGHT
A tree in summer
JULIET SNAPE

LEFT
Leaving the forest
ROBERT MACLAURIN

WE'LL NEVER SEE THE WOODS FOR THE TREES

CHRIS BAINES

YEAR AFTER YEAR we plant trees – thousands of them – perhaps even millions. Most of them die. Remember 'Plant a tree in '73'? 'Just a few sticks by '76'? Some are destroyed by vandals. Some don't even survive the journey from the shelter of the nursery to the windswept desert of the development site – they're dead on arrival. Most just fade away. They simply cannot cope with the competition for moisture as the docks and thistle, couch and groundsel crowd in around the roots.

Topsoil is a mistake. It kills them with kindness. The soil we plant our trees in is jam packed with weed seeds. We stir it up, firm it down and water it. Lucky old weeds. They love being pampered, leap a foot in the air; and leave the newly planted trees standing when it comes to grabbing the available water. All topsoil-planted trees have a struggle, but the bigger they are the more likely they are to fail. Size influences the vandals too. Make the big bold statement with a five-metre tree, protect it with stakes and guards (the ultimate deterrent), and the local lads will respond to the challenge with power-saws if necessary. When it comes to tree planting, small is beautiful.

The crazy thing is, the minute our backs are turned, the trees spring up unaided. How many of Dr Beeching's abandoned railway sidings are now sporting fine stands of silver birch? How many neglected pastures in the blighted ring of fringe farmland around our towns are burgeoning with oak and hawthorn scrub (stage one on the way to woodland)? If we want more woods, then we should learn from nature.

Encourage the birch and pussy-willow to shed their windblown seed on the soil-less rubble of our demolition sites, our stone quarries, gravel pits and railway ballast. Fence off the grazing livestock and allow the seedling scrub to sally forth from the surrounding hedgerows. If you're impatient for results, recruit the local kids to plant small seedlings, and to care for them. Nature, given time, would once more cloak the countryside with woodland. If we have lost the ability to wait for that to happen naturally, then we should use our powers to speed up the natural process. Britain was a wooded country once. Woodland could return again – but not while we keep on spreading topsoil and planting trees everywhere.

RIGHT
Gloucester Gate, Regent's Park,
February/March/April/May/June.
Oil on canvas
ADRIAN BERG

bawson   pate   grey

I am sitting alone on the edge of night
(woodcocks roding – trance dancing)
a badger comes out of the wood on ancient track
I am so close I feel sorrow for what we have done

I want to apologise – species to species,
soul to soul,
but I don't know what to say

and so must I remain
here in the distance.

DAVID HATFIELD

LEFT
The larch, Parsons Bridge
J. BAXTER
(1st prize winner, *Practical Photography* competition)

RIGHT
Tree and moon
EDMUND NAGELE

'OUR' WOOD

CAROL DAVIS

EXPERTS SAY 'OUR' WOOD could possibly date from Domesday times. Not the individual trees, you understand, but the site itself, has in all probability been continuously managed as a coppice-with-standards woodland since the heyday of the Norman forests. Then it would have been part of the forest of Feckenham, which accounted for a goodly acreage in this nook of Worcestershire. Over the centuries, 'our' wood has dwindled to a modest twelve acres; constantly retreating in the face of agricultural expansion. Like other scattered remnants of the ancient forest, 'our' wood stands islanded amid a rippling ocean of ripening grains in summer and a desert of glutinous, naked clay in winter. Sheep graze an irregular wedge of pasture on its western boundary, making occasional depredations into its lush rides and succulent young hazel rods wherever the rickety fencing once more gives way to their persistence. The Norman lords of long ago dealt strictly with such trespasses.

It pleases me to ponder that those proud Norman lords probably knew the great-great grandparents of the oaks which now punctuate the hazel stands. Treading the age-old pathways criss crossing 'our' wood, my collie bitch questing ahead for rabbits, I finger the Conservation Trust pass in my pocket; my passport to enjoy the aura of the past which filters through my imagination like sunlight through the oak leaves. Just like the deepest thickets of the wood, the distant past is an impenetrable place; even the experts are hazy as to where the truth lies. More recent times have left us records; dusty bundles of mildewed documents piled on a forgotten shelf in the Manor cellar or micro filmed in the county archives. Estate out-put expressed as the number of bundles of pea-sticks or hedging stakes cut from the hazel stools; the tally of fence-posts or cords of fuel wood sawn from the oaks; wages paid to the woodsman, repairs to his tiny cottage.

'Our' wood was actively worked by the Estate until just a few years ago when the last woodsman died. It seemed inevitable that the thread of the past would be broken but, providentially, the Conservation Trust stepped in to keep the cycle of history running smoothly through the present. The hazel is coppiced, the oaks felled and replanted, the pathways kept clear and the birds well supplied with nest boxes. On alternate Wednesdays sensible pheasants shelter elsewhere while the local syndicate – lineal descendants of the Norman hunt – exercise their shooting rights. At weekends, seeing visitors' cars parked by the entrance to 'our' wood, my bitch and I divert our walk. We savour the privacy, the intimacy, the 'stolen' pleasure of walking alone among these trees which may, who knows, hide a race memory of knights and hunting hounds, deer and wild boar. They would only remember the likes of me and my rabbiting bitch as illicit visitors, far wiser than us in the ways of 'our' wood!

LEFT
European beech
in winter aspect
DAVID MORE

OVERLEAF
Trees in a landscape,
sunrise in Essex
BARRIE E. WATTS

47